I'd rather
be fishing

Glenn Dromgoole

SOURCEBOOKS, INC.®
NAPERVILLE, ILLINOIS

Published by Sourcebooks, Inc.
P.O. Box 4410, Naperville, Illinois 60567-4410
(630) 961-3900
FAX: (630) 961-2168
www.sourcebooks.com

ISBN 1-4022-0373-X

Printed and bound in China
SNP 10 9 8 7 6 5 4 3 2 1

For Janet, whose love for fishing
got me to thinking.

Introduction

On one of my first fishing trips as a boy, my dad asked if I was having fun fishing.

"It's not the fishing I like," I am reported to have replied, "it's the catching."

However, as I have gotten older, I have come to appreciate that the process can be more satisfying than the results.

That is one of the lessons that fishing teaches us. There are many others.

I believe we can find deeper meaning in almost any activity if we try hard enough. In fishing, one doesn't have to try all that hard, actually, to find lessons of significance that apply to all of life.

We cast about for opportunities. We fish for compliments. We agonize over the prize fish that got away. We get hooked on all kinds of things, positive and negative.

Fishing is a prominent topic in the Bible and in great literature. It is an honorable occupation, a popular way to relax, a hobby, a habit, a passion. We fish, therefore, we are.

Let's get started before this gets any deeper. The text in this book is short because: (a) you would probably rather look at the pictures, and (b) you would definitely rather be fishing.

Go where the fish are.

Once when I was fishing, I kept getting my line caught in an overhead tree, which prompted my partner to remind me, "You're not going to catch many fish in a tree." The same goes for business or any other enterprise—you've got to go where the fish are if you hope to be successful.

3

The only fish that matters.

Fishing is like falling in love. As far as you're concerned, the one you're trying to reel in is the only fish in the river.

A simple formula.

If people fished more and complained less, it would be a better world.

Good for the soul.

Fishing is good for the soul. You toss your line out. You reel it in. You toss it out. You reel it in. It leaves the mind free to wander. Occasionally a fish might interrupt the reverie, but that's okay too.

Satisfaction comes from within.

Y ou've heard it said that the two happiest days in a man's life are the day he buys his first boat—and the day he sells it. Isn't that how it is in other facets of life? We think that our life will be complete and perfect if we can just acquire such-and-such. Eventually we learn, or should, that satisfaction doesn't come from things, but from within ourselves.

Clear lines.

If only life could be as simple as fishing. In fishing there are no ambiguities. Either you catch it or you don't. It's pretty clear cut. The lines of life, unlike fishing lines, are not so easily defined.

Work at it.

Fishing, like nearly anything else done well, requires more practice than theory. The best fishermen would rather fish than read about how to fish.

The thrill of the catch.

There are few simple thrills in life equal to that of hooking a fish on the other end of the line. But an even bigger thrill than catching a fish yourself is watching a child catch one. It's a thrill for two reasons—the child feels a sense of pride and accomplishment, and the parent feels a sense of relief that the fishing trip has been a success.

Take the bait.

Why not just boil and eat the shrimp, rather than use it for bait? If you have to ask that question, you just don't understand.

Favorite places.

Favorite fishing holes, like favorite restaurants or favorite places to watch a sunset, should be shared only with your closest friends.

Hooked on fishing.

When you get serious about fishing—or any other line of pursuit—you're the one hooked.

Food on the plate.

You don't have to like to eat fish to like to catch them. And vice versa, I suppose. Some of the best fishermen I've known couldn't stand to eat fish. Which illustrates a truism: that the chase is often much more rewarding than the catch.

Bones and thorns.

Personally, I love to eat fish, but I don't like all those tiny bones. Why couldn't God have made fish with a solid bone down the middle? Sure would be more convenient. Bones are to fish, I suppose, what thorns are to roses.

Tossing out a few lines.

Fishing has entered our language in ways that don't have anything to do with fish. We fish for compliments. We fish around for information. We bait an opponent in a debate. We lure someone into an argument. We toss out a line in a speech. We are told to fish or cut bait when we need to make a commitment. We bite, or fall for things hook, line, and sinker.

Peace and quiet.

I've never been convinced that it was important to be quiet when you're fishing. Do we think the fish are listening to our conversations? It's probably just a ploy by fishermen to gain themselves a little peace and quiet—which isn't a bad idea, at that.

Keep it fair.

Fishing seems such a fair sport, with the fish actually holding the edge. But putting out a trot line—stretched across the river or creek with every hook baited—unfairly shifts the advantage to the absentee landlord. Where's the satisfaction in that?

Reel in the TV.

These days, you don't even have to leave your comfortable house to go fishing. You can watch it on TV. Isn't that how we experience most sports today? Not by actually participating—just watching other people play. The good part about fishing via TV is that there aren't any mosquitoes—and there's always a bathroom close by.

The bright side.

Cleaning fish isn't the most pleasant task. But, like most things, if we look on the bright side it isn't so bad. If we hadn't been successful in catching so many fish, we wouldn't have so many to clean. We would much rather have a mess of fish to clean than no mess at all.

The grace of an expert.

Good fishermen, like experts in most fields, can't really explain what makes them good. They know what they're doing, and they just seem to do it naturally, with ease, with grace, with confidence.

Take your mind off your troubles.

Fishing gets your mind off your troubles. Your focus is on catching fish, and everything else is put on hold for a while. When you do return to reality, often you do so with a clearer perspective.

The joy of simplicity.

A cane pole and a can of worms is the low-tech version of fishing, sort of like writing on a manual typewriter or with a pad and pencil. You don't have to have a lot of expensive equipment to get the job done.

Religious symbolism.

Although a lot of fishing takes place on lakes and rivers on Sunday morning, fishing has religious significance in the Christian community. Jesus picked fishermen as disciples and used fishing analogies to illustrate points. The fish was an early Christian symbol and has enjoyed renewed popularity in recent years.

Loaves and fishes.

The little boy in the parable of feeding the five thousand had five loaves and two fishes, not two boxes of fried chicken. In the modern version, he would have five hush puppies and two fish fillets.

Lord, give me patience...

If fishing teaches any virtue especially well, it teaches patience. The fisherman can't do anything to force the fish to bite. He can only keep tossing the bait out there and wait for some action.

...and do it now!

Patience, as most fishermen know, is an overrated virtue.

Hope, faith, and fishing.

Fishing also teaches about hope and faith—hoping that the next time you toss out your line will be the one when the fish grabs it, and then actually believing that will happen.

A purpose for worms.

God obviously intended for us to fish. Otherwise, why would He have created worms?

Fish stories.

Fishing probably does not teach another virtue very well—telling the truth. The fish get bigger and more abundant the more their stories are told. Possibly that's because fishermen have to be so optimistic by nature that they begin believing what they wish to be true.

Supermarket fishing.

It's hard to justify fishing as a way to put food on the table. For most of us, it would be significantly cheaper to buy fish at the store. But where's the thrill in that?

Don't count the cost.

Fishermen don't ever stop to figure out how much per pound their catch really cost them. Or shouldn't.

Eat the bait?

As an adult, I have tried to develop a taste for sushi. But I have to keep reminding myself, "You're really not eating the bait!" And I can't help but think, "Wouldn't this be better fried?"

Not boring.

Fishing, like baseball or chess or classical music, is boring only to those who don't understand it.

Man vs. fish

I've never thought of fishing as a competitive sport—at least not until recently, with all the high-dollar bass tournaments. The competition should be between man and fish, woman and fish, kid and fish. That's the challenge, not who caught the biggest or most fish.

A fishing pond for kids.

Every town of any size ought to have a pond where kids can learn to fish—and a cadre of volunteers to teach them the fundamentals. Wouldn't that be a good job for retired folks who enjoy fishing?

Fly fishing.

There are scenic spots all over the world to experience fly fishing, but we have to make the effort and spend the money to get there. It is easier to just stay where we are, and fish the places that we know, rather than take the risk and invest the resources in new adventures.

In life, as in fishing, sometimes we need to get out of our comfort zones and expand our horizons.

No guarantees.

Deep sea fishing is best done in groups and with a guide. But don't you wish a guide had to issue a money-back guarantee that you would actually catch something worth keeping, or at least worth taking a picture of? Maybe that's the point: There are no guarantees in fishing, or in life. Just opportunities.

A passion for fishing.

If you're looking for an inexpensive hobby, don't take up fishing or golf. If you're looking for an all-consuming passion, either will do.

Fishy question.

If something is suspicious, dubious, or shady, why is it considered fishy? Maybe because it smells?

Drink like a fish.

Why is it that a heavy drinker is said to drink like a fish? Whoever heard of a drunk fish—if you don't count college freshmen?

Because they are fresh?

And why are college freshmen called fish anyway?

Stay in school.

The difference between fish and fishermen is that fish stay in schools as long as they can.

Course for success.

Given the number of corporate executives who enjoy the sport, perhaps a college course in fly fishing should be required for business administration majors. Not a bad idea for the rest of us as well.

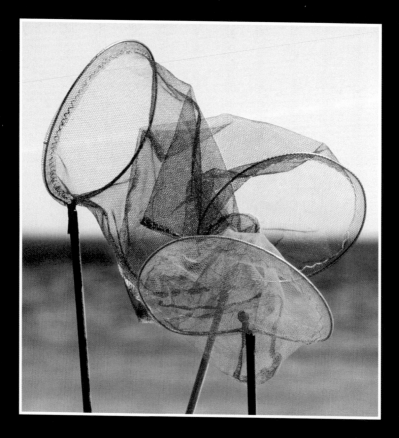

Net worth.

When a fisherman asks, "What is your net worth?" he's not asking how much stock you own.

The one that got away.

The one that got away always seems to get exaggerated as the years pass— and not just in fishing. The opportunity that got away; the championship game that was lost; the idea that somebody else developed; the job that somebody else was in the right place for, at the right time. The best rule is not to dwell on the ones that got away, and make the most of the ones that didn't.

About the Author

Glenn Dromgoole is the author of ten books, including the bestselling *What Happy Dogs Know* and *What Dogs Teach Us.*

He is managing editor of McWhiney Foundation Press and State House Press, which publishes books on Texas and Civil War history, writes a column on Texas books and authors, and chairs the West Texas Book and Author Festival.

Photo Credits